The Holy Gospel of John

A new translation
by
Peter Levi

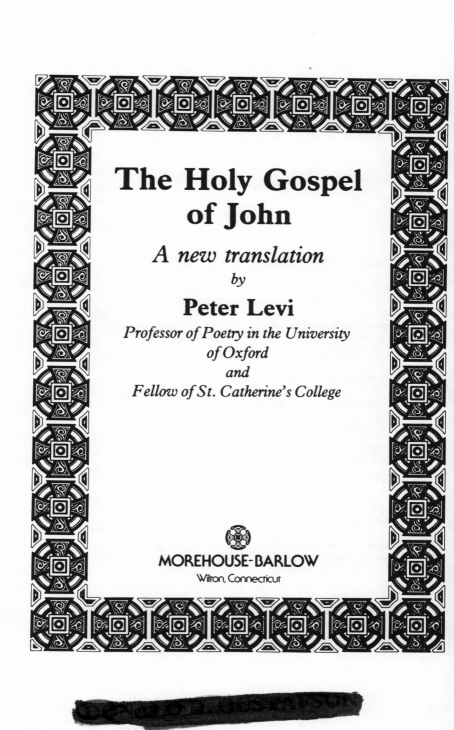

The Holy Gospel of John

A *new translation*
by

Peter Levi
Professor of Poetry in the University of Oxford
and
Fellow of St. Catherine's College

MOREHOUSE-BARLOW
Wilton, Connecticut

First published in Great Britain by Churchman Publishing Limited

First American edition published by

Morehouse-Barlow Co. Inc.
    78 Danbury Road
Wilton, Connecticut 06897

Cover design by Carole Masonberg

Library of Congress Cataloging-in-Publication Data

Bible. N. T. John. English. Levi. 1988.
    The Holy Gospel of John.

    Reprint. Originally published: Worthing, Eng.:
Churchman Pub., 1985.
    I. Levi, Peter. II. Title.
BS2613   1988b   226'.50529   88-14720

ISBN: 0-8192-1427-2

Printed in the United States of America
by
BSC LITHO
Harrisburg, PA

TRANSLATOR'S NOTE

This version is not intended to replace old versions. Its purpose is to convey the exact sense, and as far as possible the precise tone of the original, in modern vernacular English. In some ways it is closer to John's Greek usage than it is to normal English. Bible translations have often taken a similar liberty in the past. Rough Greek makes rough English. I debated a long time over words with several meanings, and about the normal, smooth sequence of tenses in English, but I did not find absolute consistency attractive. My only hope is that this version will convey a neglected quality, and speak with immediacy as the Gospel was intended to speak, and did speak to its first readers. All versions of the Gospel cover up twists and complexities of the original languages of Christianity. The task of explaining them belongs to theologians. Mere translations should be as simple as possible, particularly in our language at this time of day.   P.L.

THE HOLY GOSPEL OF JOHN

CHAPTER 1

In the beginning the word was, and the word was God's, and the word was God. He was of God in the beginning. All things came to be through him, and without him nothing at all came to be. What came to be in him was life, and that life was the light of mankind. And the light shines in the darkness and the darkness has not overshadowed it. A man was born who was sent from God, his name was John. He came as a witness, to be a witness about the light, so that through him everyone might believe. He was not the light, he came as a witness about the light. It was the true light which enlightens every man who comes into the world. He was in the world, and through him the world was, and the world did not know him. He came to his own, and his own did not accept him. To those who did accept him, he gave the power to become children of God: to those who believe in his name, who were not begotten from blood or from the will of the flesh or from the will of man, but begotten from God. And the word became flesh and lived among us, and we saw his glory, the glory of the only son of the father: full of grace and truth. John is a witness about him, he cried out these words: I said of this man, He who shall come after me came before me, because he was first above me. Because we have all taken from his fullness, and grace upon grace. Because the law was given through Moses; grace and truth came through Jesus Christ. No one has ever seen God; his only son, who is on his father's lap, has told us about him.

And this is the witness of John, when the Jews sent him out priests and Levites from Jerusalem, to ask him, Who are you? And he admitted, he did not deny it, he admitted, I am not the Christ. And they asked him, Then what are you? Are you Elias? And he said, I am not. Are you the prophet? And he answered, No. So they said to him, Who are you? So that we can give an answer to those who sent us. What do you say about yourself? He said, I am a voice crying out in the wilderness. Make a straight road for the Lord, as Isaiah the prophet said. They had been sent by the Pharisees, and they asked him, they said to him, Then why do you baptize, if you are not the Christ, or Elias, or the prophet? John answered them, he said, I baptize in water, there is someone you do not know standing among you, who shall come after me; I am not worthy to untie his sandal-straps. All this happened in Bethabara beyond the Jordan, where John was baptizing.

The next day he sees Jesus coming towards him, and he says, Look, the lamb of God, who carries the sin of the world. This is the man of whom I said, He who was before me shall come after me because he was first above me. And I did not know him, but this is why I come to baptize with water, so that he will be revealed to Israel. And John gave witness, he said, I have seen the Spirit coming down like a dove out of heaven, and it remained on him. And I did not know him, but he who sent me to baptize with water, he said to me, When you see the Spirit come down on a man and remain on him, that is the one who baptizes with the Holy Spirit. And I have seen it and I am a witness that this is the son of God.

The next day John stood there again with two of his disciples, and looking at Jesus as he passed by, he said, Look, the lamb of God. And the two disciples heard him speak and followed Jesus. Jesus turned round and saw them following, and he says to them What are you looking for? They said to him Rabbi – which in Greek is Master – Where do you live? He says to them, Come and see. So they came and saw where he lived, and they stayed with him that day. It was about five in the evening. One of the two who heard from John and followed him was Andrew, the brother of Simon Peter. He finds his own brother Simon first, and says to him, We have found the Messias, which in Greek is Christ. They brought him to Jesus. Jesus looked at him and said, You are Simon the son of John, you shall be called Kephas, which in our language is Peter.

The next day he wanted to go out into Galilee, and he finds Philip; and Jesus says to him, Follow me. Philip was from Bethsaida, Andrew's and Peter's city. Philip finds Nathanael, and says to him, We have found the man Moses wrote about in the law, and the prophets wrote about, Jesus of Nazareth, the son of Joseph. And

9

Nathanael said to him, Can something good come from Nazareth? Philip says to him, Come and see. Jesus saw Nathanael coming towards him, and he says of him, Look, a real Israelite with no deception in him. Nathanael says to him, How do you know me? Jesus answered, he said to him, Before Philip called you, when you were under the fig-tree, I saw you. Nathanael answered him, Rabbi, you are the son of the God, you are the king of Israel. Jesus answered, he said to him, Because I told you that I saw you underneath the fig-tree, do you believe? You shall see greater things than that. And he says to him, Indeed, indeed, I tell you all, you shall see heaven opened, and the angels of God ascending and descending over the son of man.

CHAPTER 2

And on the third day there was a wedding at Kana in Galilee, and the mother of Jesus was there. And Jesus and his disciples were invited to the wedding. And as wine was wanting the mother of Jesus says to him, They have no wine. Jesus says to her, What has that to do with you and me, Madam? My time has not come yet. His mother says to the servants, Do whatever he tells you. There were six stone waterpots there, set up for the purification of the Jews, that held two or three jugs each. Jesus says to them, Fill the waterpots with water. So they filled them to the top. And he says to them, Now draw it, and take it to the master of ceremonies. And they took it to him. The master of ceremonies tasted water that had turned into wine, and he had no idea where it had come from, though the servants who drew the water knew; so the master of ceremonies calls to the bridegroom and says to him, Everyone serves the good wine first, and when people are merry then they serve less good wine: you have kept the good wine till now. Jesus did this, which was the beginning of his signs, at Kana in Galilee; and he revealed his glory, and his disciples believed in him.

After that he went down to Kapernaoum, with his mother and his brothers and his disciples, and they stayed there for a few days.

And the Jewish Passover was coming, so Jesus went up to Jerusalem. And he found people selling cattle and sheep and pigeons in the sanctuary, and the money-changers sitting at business; so he made a whip out of cords and threw them all out of the sanctuary, sheep and cattle and all, and he flung down the money of the moneychangers and overturned their tables; and he said to the pigeon-sellers, Take these out of here, do not make my father's house into a house of business. His disciples remembered that it was written, The rage of your house is eating me up. So the Jews answered, and they said to him, What sign are you showing us, when you do this? Jesus answered, and he said to them, Pull down this temple, and in three days I will raise it up. So the Jews said to him, This temple took forty-six years to build, and you will raise it up in three days? But he spoke of the temple of his body. So when he rose from the dead, his disciples remembered that he said this, and they believed in the scripture and in the word Jesus had spoken.

While he was in Jerusalem at Passover at the festival, many people saw the signs he did and believed in his name. But Jesus did not trust himself to them, because he knew them all; he had no need for anyone to inform him about man; he knew what was in man.

CHAPTER 3

There was a man who was a Pharisee, whose name was Nikodemos, he was a Jewish magistrate. He came to him at night, and said to him, Rabbi, we know that you come from God as a teacher, because no one can do the signs that you do if God is not with him. Jesus answered him, he said, Indeed, indeed, I tell you, if a man is not born from above, he cannot see the kingdom of God. Nikodemos says to him, How can a man be born when he is old? He cannot go back into his mother's womb again to be born? Jesus answered, Indeed, indeed, I tell you, if a man is not born from water and Spirit, he cannot enter the kingdom of God. What is born from flesh is flesh, and what is born from spirit is spirit. Do not be amazed because I said to you, You must all be born from above. The spirit breathes where it wishes and you hear its voice, but you have no idea where it comes from or where it goes. Every man born from the spirit is like that. Nikodemos answered, he said to him, How can that be? Jesus answered, he said to him, You are the teacher of Israel and you do not know? Indeed, indeed, I tell you, we speak about what we know and we witness to what we have seen: and you do not accept our evidence. If I said earthly things to you and you do not believe me, how will you ever believe if I say heavenly things? And no one has ever gone up into heaven except the son of man who came down out of heaven, who is in heaven. And as Moses lifted up the snake in the desert, so the son of man must be lifted up, so that everyone who believes in him has everlasting life.

Because God so loved the world that he gave his only son, so that everyone who believes in him will not perish, but have everlasting life. Because God did not send his son into the world to judge the world, but for the world to be saved through him. The man that believes in him is not judged, the man that does not believe has already been judged, because he has not believed in the name of the only son of God. This is the judgement: the light has come into the world, and men loved the darkness more than the light, because what they were doing was evil. Everyone who behaves badly hates the light, he does not come to the light, so that his deeds are not tested. But the man who does right comes to the light so that his deeds are clearly seen: that they were done in God.

After that Jesus and his disciples came into the Judaean country, and there he lived with them and baptized. John was baptizing too, in Ainon near Saleim, where there was abundant water, and the people came and were baptized, because John had not yet been thrown into prison. A discussion started up between John's disciples and a Jew about purification. So they came to John and said to him, Rabbi, that man who was with you beyond Jordan, the one for whom you gave witness, look at him, he is baptizing, and they are all going to him. John answered, he said, A man cannot take anything at all, except what is granted to him by heaven. You yourselves are my witnesses that I said, I am not the Christ, but I am sent ahead of him. The one who has the bride is the bridegroom, but the bridegroom's friend, who stands and listens for him, is delighted at the sound of the bridegroom's voice. So my delight has been fulfilled. He must grow greater and I must grow smaller.

He who comes down from above is over all men. He who comes from earth is earthly, and his language is earthly. He who comes down from heaven is over all men. He witnesses to what he has seen and heard, and no one accepts his witness. Whoever has accepted his witness has given his seal that God is true. For the one whom God has sent speaks the words of God; the Spirit does not give by halves and quarters. The Father loves the Son, and has given everything into his hand. Whoever believes in the Son has everlasting life, and whoever disbelieves in the Son shall not see life, but the anger of God remains with him.

CHAPTER 4

So when Jesus knew that the Pharisees had heard he was making more disciples and baptizing more people than John, although it was not Jesus himself who was baptizing, but his disciples, he left Judaea and went back again into Galilee. He had to pass through Samaria. So he comes to a city in Samaria called Sychar, near the village that Jacob gave to his son Joseph; Jacob's well was there. So Jesus was tired out from the road, and he was sitting down by the well. It was late afternoon. A woman from Samaria comes to draw water. Jesus says to her, Give me a drink. His disciples had gone off to the city to buy food. So the Samaritan woman says to him, How can you be asking me for a drink, you being a Jew and me being a Samaritan woman? Jews have nothing to do with Samaritans. Jesus answered: he said to her, If you knew the gift of God, and who is saying to you Give me a drink, you would be asking him, and he would have given you living water. The woman says to him Sir, you haven't even got a bucket, and the well is deep; where have you got living water from? Are you greater than our father Jacob who gave us the well, and drank from it himself, and so did his sons and his flocks? Jesus answered, and he said to her: Everyone who drinks this water will be thirsty again, but whoever drinks the water I shall give him will never be thirsty again, but the water I shall give him will become a spring of water in him, leaping up to everlasting life. The woman says to him, Sir, give me this water, so that I shan't be thirsty and shan't come here to draw water. Jesus says to her, Go and call your husband, and come back here. The woman answered, she said to him, I have no husband. Jesus says to her, You are right to say I have no husband. You have had five husbands, and now the one you have is not your husband. You have told the truth. The woman says to him, Sir, I see you are a prophet. Our fathers worshipped on this mountain, and yet others say that the proper place for worship is Jerusalem. Jesus says to her, Believe me woman, the time is coming when you shall worship your father neither on this mountain nor in Jerusalem. You are worshipping what you have not known, we are worshipping what we have known, because salvation comes from the Jews. But the time is coming and is here now, when true worshippers will worship their father in spirit and in truth; because that is the kind of worshippers he is looking for. God is spirit, and his worshippers should worship him in spirit and in truth. The woman says to him, I know the Messias is coming, who is called Christ; when he comes he will tell us everything. Jesus says to her, I am him, it is me talking to you.

And at this moment his disciples arrived, and they were amazed he was talking with a woman. Still, no one said What are you wanting? or Why are you talking with her? So the woman left her water-pot and went off to the city, and she says to the people, Come along, and see a man who has told me everything I ever did. Is this not Christ? They came out from the city, and they came to him. In the meanwhile his disciples were asking questions. Eat, Rabbi, they say, and he says to them, I have food to eat you do not know. So his disciples were saying to each other, Has someone brought him food? Jesus says to them, My food is for me to do his will that sent me, and to finish his work. Do you not say, There are four months to go but harvest time is coming? Look, I tell you, lift up your eyes and look at the countryside, it is white for harvest now. The reaper takes his wages and gathers in a harvest for eternal life, to make the sower and the reaper glad together. Because in this the saying is true that one man sows and another man reaps. I have sent you out to reap what you have not worked hard to produce. Others have worked hard, and you have taken over from their work.

Many of the Samaritans from that city believed in him because of what the woman said, He told me everything I ever did. So when the Samaritans came to him, they asked him to stay with them, and he did stay there for two days. And many more believed because of his words, and they said to the woman, We no longer believe because of what you said: we have heard for ourselves and we know that this is the saviour of the world.

After those two days he left that place to go into Galilee. Because Jesus himself declared that a prophet gets no respect in his own country. So when he came into Galilee, the Galilaeans accepted him, they had seen all he did in Jerusalem at the festival, because they had been to the festival as well.

So he came back to Kana in Galilee where he turned

the water into wine. And there was a minister of the King whose son was ill at Kapernaoum. When this man heard that Jesus had come from Judaea into Galilee, he went out to him and asked him to come down and cure his son, who was dying. So Jesus said to him, You will not believe unless you see miraculous signs and unnatural wonders. So the King's minister says to him, Sir, come with me before my young son dies. Jesus says to him, Go on your way, your son is alive. The man believed these words that Jesus said to him, and went away. When he was still on his way home his slaves came to meet him and said his son was still alive. So he found out from them the time when the boy got well. They said the fever dropped away from him yesterday an hour after midday. So the father understood that it was just at the time when Jesus said to him, Your son is alive; and he believed, and his whole house and family believed. That was the second sign that Jesus performed when he came into Galilee from Judaea.

CHAPTER 5

After that there was a Jewish festival, and Jesus went up to Jerusalem.

By the sheepfolds in Jerusalem there is a bath, which is called Bethesda in Hebrew and has five colonnades. A vast assembly of afflicted people, the blind and the crippled and the withered were lying there waiting for the movement of the water, because sometimes an angel of God came down into the bath and disturbed the water, and the first to go in after the disturbance of the water got well from whatever disease he might have. There was a man there sick with the same disease for thirty-eight years. Jesus saw him lying there and knew he had been there all that long time, so he says to him, Do you want to get well? The afflicted man answered him, Sir, I have nobody to put me in the bath when the water stirs. While I am getting there someone else goes in before me. So Jesus says to him, Get up, pick up your bed, and walk. And at once the man got well, and he lifted up his bed, and he walked.

It was Sabbath on that day. So the Jews said to the man who was cured, This is Sabbath, you are not allowed to carry your bed. So he answered them, The man who made me well told me to pick up my bed and walk. They asked him, Who was it who said pick it up and walk? The man who was cured did not know who it was, because the place being crowded Jesus had gone away.

Afterwards, Jesus finds him in the temple, and says to him, Look, you have got well; do nothing wrong any more, in case something worse happens to you. The man went away and told the Jews that it was Jesus who made him well. And because of that the Jews went after Jesus for doing that on a Sabbath. But Jesus answered them, My father goes on with his work up to this minute, and so am I doing my work. So because of this the Jews wanted to kill him all the more because he not only did away with the Sabbath, but he called God his own father as well, which made him equal to God.

So Jesus answered, and he said to them, Indeed I say to you, indeed, the son can do nothing of his own, unless he sees his father doing it; because whatever the father does the son does it too, just like him. Because the father loves his son, and shows him what he does himself. And he will show him greater doings than this, so that you wonder at it. Because just as the father raises up the dead and brings them to life, the son also brings to life those he chooses. And the father does not judge anybody, he has given all power of judging to his son, so that everyone honours the son as they honour the father. Whoever gives no honours to the son gives none to the father who sent him. Indeed I say to you, indeed, whoever hears my words and believes in the one that sent me has everlasting life, he will not come to judgement, he has passed over from death into life. Indeed I say to you, indeed, the time is coming and is here now when the dead will hear the voice of the son of God, and those who hear it will live. Because just as the father has life in himself, he has given it to his son as well, to have life in himself. And he gave him authority to judge because he is a son of mankind. Do not be amazed at that, because the time is coming when all those in the graves will hear his voice and come out from them, those who did good to a resurrection of life, and those who did evil to a resurrection of condemnation.

I am not able to do anything of my own; I judge as I am told, and my judgement is just, because I am not looking for my own will but his will that sent me. If I am my own witness, my declaration is not true. Someone else is my witness, and I know the declaration he makes about me is true. You sent off to John, and he witnessed to the truth. I am not taking the declaration of a human witness, I am saying this for you to be saved. He was the burning and the shining light, and you wanted to be happy for a while in his light. But I have a greater declaration than John's because the things that my father gave me to finish, the things that I do, are witnesses for me, that it was my father who sent me. And the father who sent me has been a witness for me. You have never heard his voice nor seen his shape. And you have not got his word dwelling in you because you do not believe in the person he sent. You search the holy books because you think you have everlasting life in them, and yet the holy books are witnesses for me, but you do not want to come to me and live. But I understand you; you have not got the love of God in you. I have come in the name of my father, and you do not accept me; if someone else should come in his own name, you will accept him. How can you believe, when you accept approval from one another and never look for the honour that comes from

God alone? Do not think that I shall accuse you to my father. You have your accuser, Moses, in whom you have hoped. Because if you had believed Moses, you would have believed me. But if you don't believe his writings, how will you believe my sayings?

CHAPTER 6

After that Jesus went away across the sea of Galilee, Lake Tiberias. There was a big crowd following him, because they had seen the miraculous signs he performed over the sick. But Jesus went up onto the mountain and sat there with his disciples. It was near the Jewish festival of Passover. So Jesus raised his eyes and saw there was a big crowd coming out to him, and he says to Philip, Where shall we buy bread, for these people to eat? He was saying it to test him, because he knew what he was going to do. Philip answered him, Two hundred dinars worth of bread will not be enough for them, if every one of them takes a little piece. One of the disciples, Simon Peter's brother Andrew, says to him, There is a young boy here with five barley loaves and two fishes, but what is that among so many? Jesus said, Make the people lie down. There was plenty of grass there. So as many as five thousand men lay down. So Jesus took the loaves and offered thanks and handed them round to the people lying there, and in the same way as much as they wanted from the fishes. When they were full up, he says to his disciples, collect up the bits that are left over, so that nothing is lost. So they collected, and they filled twelve baskets of bits of the five barley loaves left over from eating. So when the people saw the miraculous sign he had given, they said, This man is truly the prophet who is coming into the world.

So Jesus realized they were going to come and take him and make him king, and he went away onto the mountain alone.

When evening came, his disciples came down to the sea and got into a boat; they set out over the sea to Kapernaoum. And it was already dark, and Jesus had not come to them yet, and the sea was disturbed with a big wind blowing. When they had gone three or four miles or so, they see Jesus walking on the water, coming close to the boat, and they were terrified. He says to them, It's me. Don't be frightened. So they wanted to take him into the boat. And suddenly the boat was at the shore they were headed for.

The next day the crowd that had gathered on the far shore could see there was no boat except the one, and they saw Jesus had not gone in the boat with his disciples, his disciples had gone away alone. Other boats came out from Tiberias, close to the place where the Master offered thanks and they ate the bread. So when the crowd saw that Jesus was not there, and nor were his disciples, they got into these other boats, and came to Kapernaoum looking for Jesus. And when they found him on the opposite shore, they said to him, Rabbi, when did you get here? Jesus answered them, and he said, Indeed I tell you, indeed you are looking for me not because you saw miraculous signs, but because you ate the bread and you got full. What you should work for is not the food that perishes but the food that remains for an everlasting lifetime, which the son of mankind will give you. Because the father has put his seal on him, by the father I mean God. So they said to him, What shall we do to work at the works of God? Jesus answered, and he said to them, this is the work of God, believe in the one he sent. So they said to him, So what miraculous sign do you give, for us to see and believe in you? What is your work? Our fathers ate the manna in the desert, as it is written, He gave them bread to eat from heaven. So Jesus said to them, Indeed I tell you, indeed it was not Moses who gave you the bread out of heaven, but my father gives you the true bread of heaven, because the bread of God is what comes down out of heaven and gives life to the world. So they said to him, Sir, give us this bread always. Jesus said to them, I am the bread of life. Whoever comes to me will not be hungry, and whoever believes in me will never thirst. But I told you that you have seen me and still you do not believe. Everything my father gives me shall come to me, and I will not throw anyone out who comes to me. Because I have come down from heaven not to do my own will but his will that sent me. And this is his will that sent me, that out of all he has given me, I should destroy nothing, but raise it up on the last day. Because this is my father's will, for everyone who sees his son and believes in him to have everlasting life. And I will raise him up on the last day.

So the Jews were muttering about him, because he said, I am the bread that came down from heaven. And they said, Is this not Jesus son of Joseph, whose father and mother we know? How can he say now, I have come down out of heaven? Jesus answered, and he said to them, Stop muttering to one another. No one can come to me unless the father who sent me drags him, and I will raise him up on the last day. It is written in the prophets, And they shall all be taught by God. Everyone who has heard from my father and learnt from him comes to me. Not that anyone has seen the father except the one that comes from God, he has seen the father. Indeed I tell you, indeed, whoever believes has everlasting life. I am the bread of life. Your fathers ate the manna in the desert, and they died. This is the bread that comes down out of heaven, so that people shall eat it and not die. I am the living bread that came down out of heaven. If anyone eats this bread, he shall live for all eternity. And the bread I shall give is my body for the life of the world.

So the Jews were fighting among themselves, saying How can this man give us his body to eat? So Jesus said to them, Indeed I tell you, indeed, unless you eat the body of the son of man and drink his blood, you have no life in you. Whoever eats my body and drinks my blood has everlasting life, and I shall raise him up on the last day. Because my body is true food, and my blood is true drink. Whoever eats my body and drinks my blood remains in me, and I remain in him. As the living father sent me, so I live through the father, and whoever eats me will live through me. This is the bread that came down out of heaven, not as our fathers ate and they died; whoever eats this bread will live for all eternity. He said these words teaching in the synagogue at Kapernaoum.

When they heard it, many of his disciples said, That is a hard saying, who can listen to it? But Jesus knew in himself that his disciples were muttering about it, and he said to them, Does this offend you? What if you see the son of man ascending to where he was? The spirit is lifegiving, the body is no use. The sentences I have spoken to you are spirit and life. But there are some of you who do not believe. Because Jesus knew from the beginning who the non-believers were, and who was going to betray him. And he said, That is why I told you that no one can come to me unless it is granted to him by my father.

From that moment, many of his disciples went away and they left him, they no longer went around with him. So Jesus said to the twelve, Do you want to go as well? Simon Peter answered him, Master, who are we to go to? You have words of everlasting life. And we have believed and we have understood that you are the Holy one of God. Jesus answered them, Have I not picked out you twelve for myself, and yet one of you is a devil? He meant Judas son of Simon of Iskaria. That is who was going to betray him, one of those twelve.

CHAPTER 7

And after that Jesus walked about in Galilee. He did not want to go about in Judaea, because the Jews were thinking of killing him. The festival of the Jews called the Tabernacles was near. So his brothers said to him, Leave this place and go into Judaea, so that your disciples can see the things you do as others have seen. Because no one does a thing secretly if he is trying to be talked about freely and openly. If you do these things, make yourself plain to the world. Not even his brothers believed in him. So Jesus says to them, My time has not come yet, but your time is always ready for you. The world cannot hate you; it hates me, because I am a witness against it that what it does is evil. You go up to the festival; I am not going up for this festival, because my hour has not struck yet. With those words to them, he remained in Galilee.

But when his brothers went up for the festival, then he went up too, only not openly but secretly, so to speak. So the Jews were looking for him at the festival, and they were saying, Where is that man? And there was a lot of muttering about him in the crowds. Some of them were saying, He is good, but others said No, he is deceiving the crowd. But no one spoke out openly about him for fear of the Jews. Then, when the festival was at its height, Jesus came up to the temple and taught there. So the Jews said in amazement, How does this man

31

know letters, when he never learnt? So Jesus answered them, and he said, My teaching is not my own, but his that sent me. Anyone that will do his will understands this teaching, as to whether it comes from God or whether I speak for myself. One who speaks for himself is looking for his own glory, but one who looks for his glory that sent him is genuine, there is no injustice in him. Did Moses not give you the law, and yet none of you does what the law says? Why are you wanting to kill me? The crowd answered, You have a devil in you; who wants to kill you? Jesus answered, and he said to them, I have done one thing, and you are all amazed. And so Moses gave you circumcision (not that it comes from Moses, it comes from your ancestors), and yet you circumcise a man on the Sabbath. If a man gets his circumcision on a Sabbath, so that the law of Moses is kept, are you angry with me because I made a whole man healthy on the Sabbath? Do not judge by appearances, make a just judgement.

So some of the Jerusalemites were saying, Is this not the man they want to kill? And look, he speaks quite openly, and they say nothing to him. Is it possible the governors really know that this is Christ? But we know where this man comes from, and when Christ comes, no one knows where he comes from. So Jesus cried out as he taught in the temple, and he said, You know me and you know where I come from; and I have not come from myself, he who sent me is truthful, you do not know him. I know him because I am from him and he sent me. So they tried to take him, yet no one layed a hand on him, because his time had not come. But many in the crowd believed in him, and they were saying, Will Christ when he comes do more miraculous signs than this man has done? The Pharisees heard the crowd muttering like this about him, and the chief priests and the Pharisees sent their men to take him. So Jesus said, I am with you for a little time yet, then I am going to him that sent me. You will look for me, and not find me, and you cannot come where I am. So the Jews said to themselves, Where is he going to go, where we shall not find him? Can he be going abroad among the Greek Jews, to teach the Greeks? What did those words mean, when he said, You will look for me and not find me, and you cannot come where I am?

On the last and great day of the festival, Jesus stood and cried out, and said, If anyone is thirsty, let him come to me and let him drink. Whoever believes in me, as the Bible said, rivers of living water shall run out of his belly. He was speaking of the Spirit which those that believed in him would receive. The Spirit had not come yet, because Jesus was not glorified yet. So people in the crowd who heard these words were saying, This man really is the prophet. Others were saying, This is Christ. Others again said, Does Christ not come from Galilee? Did the Bible not say that Christ comes from the seed of David and from Bethlehem, the village where David lived? So the crowd was divided about him. Some of them wanted to take him, but no one layed hands on him.

So the servants of the high priests and the Pharisees returned to them, and the high priests and the Pharisees said, Why have you not brought him? Their servants answered, No man has ever spoken like this. So the

Pharisees answered them. Can you have been deceived as well? Has any of the governors believed in him, or any of the Pharisees? But this crowd that has no knowledge of the law is cursed and damned. Nikodemos says to them (Nikodemos who came to him earlier and who was one of them), Does our law judge the man without hearing him first and seeing the things he does? They replied and said to him, Can you be from Galilee as well? Study it and you will see that no prophet arises in Galilee. And they all went away to their own houses.

CHAPTER 8

But Jesus went to the hill of olive trees. And at dawn he reappeared in the temple and all the people came to him. And he sat and taught them. And the scholars and the Pharisees bring in a woman arrested for adultery, and they stand her in the middle and say to him, Teacher, this woman has been caught in the act of adultery. In the law, Moses commanded us to stone women like that; so what do you say about her? They were saying this to test him, so as to have something to charge him with. But Jesus bent down and wrote with his finger in the earth. And when they went on questioning him, he looked up and said to them, Whoever of you all has done no sin, let him be the first to throw a stone at her. And he bent down and wrote again with his finger in the earth. And when they heard him they went away one by one, beginning with the oldest until they were all gone. And Jesus was left alone with the woman who was in the middle. And Jesus looked up and said to her, Lady, where are they? Has no one condemned you? And she said, No one Sir. And Jesus said to her, Nor do I condemn you. Go on your way. Do no more sinning from now on.

So Jesus spoke to them again and said, I am the light of the world. No follower of mine will walk in the dark, he will have the light of life. So the Pharisees said to him, You are making a statement about yourself, and the statement is not true. Jesus answered and he said to them, And even if I make a statement about myself, what I say is true: because I know where I came from, and where I am going. You do not know where I came from, or where I am going. You judge by the body, but I am not judging anyone. And even if I do judge, my judgement is true, because I am not alone, but I and the father that sent me judge together. And it is written in your law that the evidence of two people is true. I give evidence about myself, and the father that sent me gives evidence about me. So they said to him, Where is your father? Jesus answered, You have not known me nor my father; if you had known me, you would have known my father. He spoke these sentences in the treasury, when he was teaching in the temple. And no one arrested him, because his time had not come.

He said to them another time, I am going, and you will search for me, and you will die in your sin. Where I am going, you cannot come. So the Jews were saying, Is he going to kill himself then, since he says Where I am going, you cannot come? And he said to them, You are from below, I am from above; you are from this world, I am not from this world. So I said to you that you will die in your sins. Because if you do not believe what I am, you will die in your sins. So they said to him, What are you? Jesus said to them, I am the beginning, and I am speaking to you. I have much to say about you and to judge in you. He that sent me is truthful, and what I speak to the world is what I have heard from him. They did not understand he was telling them about his father. So Jesus said, When you lift up the son of man, then you will see what I am; I do nothing of my own, but I speak as my father taught me. And he that sent me is with me, he has not left me alone; because I always do what pleases him. When he said this many believed in him.

So Jesus said to those Jews who believed in him, If you stay with my words, you are really my disciples; and you will see the truth, and the truth will set you free. They answered him, We are the seed of Abraham, and we have never been slaves to anyone; what do you mean by You will be set free? Jesus answered them, Indeed I tell you, indeed, everyone who does a sin is a slave of sin. The slave does not stay in the house for ever, the son stays there for ever. So if the son sets you free, you will be genuinely free. I know you are the seed of Abraham, but you want to kill me, because my words have no room in you. I say the things I have seen with my father, and you are doing the things you have heard from your father. They answered him and they said, Our father is Abraham. Jesus says to them, If you are Abraham's children, you are doing Abraham's work. But now you are wanting to kill me, when I told you the truth, which I heard from God; that is not Abraham's work. You are doing your father's work. They said to him, We were not born in a brothel, we have one father. God is our father. Jesus said to them, If God were your father you you would love me, because I came from God and I come from God; I have not come from myself, God sent me. Why do you not recognize my voice? Because you are not capable of hearing what I say. You come from your father the devil, and you want to carry out your father's wishes. He was a murderer of men from the beginning, he has never lived with truth, because there is no truth in him. When he tells his lie he says what is in him, because he is a liar and the father of the lie. And because I tell you the truth, you do not believe me. Which of you will prove me wrong about sin? If I am speaking the truth, why do you not believe me? Whoever is from God listens to the sayings of God, that is why you do not hear them, because you are not from God. The Jews answered, and they said to him, Are we not right to say you are a Samarian and you have a devil in you? Jesus answered, I have no devil in me, but I honour my father, and you dishonour me. I am not looking for my own glory, there is one who seeks it, there is one who judges. Indeed I tell you, indeed, if anyone keeps my words he will not see death for all eternity. The Jews said to him, Now we can see you have a devil in you. Abraham died, and the prophets died, and yet you say, If anyone keeps my words he will not taste death for all eternity. Are you any greater than our father Abraham, who died? And the prophets died. Who do you reckon you are? Jesus answered, If I glorify myself my glory is nothing. It is my father who glorifies me: you say he is your God, and yet you do not know him. But I know him, and if I say I have not known him I shall be a liar, like you. I do know him, and I keep his words. Your father Abraham was glad to see my days, and he did see them and was happy. So the Jews said to him, You are not fifty years old yet and you saw Abraham? Jesus said to them, Indeed I tell you indeed, before Abraham was, I am. So they picked up stones to throw at him, but Jesus hid himself and went out of the temple.

CHAPTER 9

And as he passed by, he saw a man blind from birth. And his disciples asked him, Rabbi, who has sinned, this man or his parents, for him to be born blind? Jesus answered, Neither the man nor his parents; it was so that God's work should be plainly seen in him. We must do his work that sent me, while the daylight lasts. The night is coming, no one can work then. While I am in the world, I am the light of the world. When he had said that he spat on the ground, and made mud with his spit, and smeared the mud on the man's eyes, and said to him, Go and wash in the bath of Siloam (which means Sent). He went away then and washed, and came out seeing. So his neighbours, and people who had seen him before as a beggar, were saying, Is this not the man that used to sit and beg? Some were saying, This is him; others were saying No, but he looks like him; but the man himself said, I am him. So they said to him, Then how were your eyes opened? He answered, The man called Jesus made mud and smeared my eyes, and he told me, Go to Siloam and wash. So I went and washed and then I could see. And they said to him, Where is he? He says, I do not know.

They take him to the Pharisees, this man who used to be blind. It was Sabbath on the day when Jesus made mud and opened his eyes. So they asked him again and the Pharisees asked him as well, how he got his sight.

He told them, He put mud on my eyes, and I washed, and I can see. So some of the Pharisees were saying, This man is not from God, because he does not keep the Sabbath. But others were saying, How can a sinful man work miraculous signs like these? And they were divided. So they speak to the blind man again, What do you say about him, since he opened your eyes? He said, I say he is a prophet. The Jews did not believe that the man was blind and got his sight until they called for his parents and questioned them, and said Is this your son who you say was born blind? So how can he see now? The man's parents answered and they said, We know this is our son, and we know he was born blind; as to how he can see now, we have no knowledge. Whether somebody opened his eyes or not we have no knowledge. Ask him, he is old enough, he will speak for himself. His parents said that for fear of the Jews, because the Jews had already agreed that if anyone admitted this was Christ, that person should be expelled from their community and their nation. That was why his parents said, He is old enough, you can question him. So they called in the man who was blind a second time, and they said to him, Give glory to God. We know that this man is sinful. So he answered, I do not know whether he is sinful, I only know one thing, I know I was blind and now I can see. So they said to him, What did he do to you? How did he open your eyes? He answered them, I have already told you, and you did not listen; why do you want to hear it again? Do you want to become his disciples too? And they abused him, and they said, You are his disciple, we are disciples of Moses. We know that God spoke to Moses; we do not know where this man comes from. The man answered, and he said to them, That is what is surprising in all this: the fact that you do not know where he comes from, even though he opened my eyes. We know God does not listen to sinners, but if someone lives religiously and carries out God's wishes, then God listens to that man. It has never been heard of that anyone ever opened the eyes of a man born blind. If this man were not from God, he would not have had the power to do anything. So they replied, and they said to him, You were born in sins from head to foot, and are you teaching us? And they threw him out.

Jesus heard they had thrown him out, so he went and found him and said, Do you believe in the son of God? The man replied and said, And who is he, Master, and I will believe in him? Jesus said to him, You have not only seen him, he is talking to you now. So he said, I believe, Master, and he fell at his feet and worshipped him. And Jesus said, I came into this world for a judgement, to make the sightless see and the sighted blind. Those of the Pharisees who were with him heard this, and they said to him, So are we blind? Jesus said to them, If you were blind you would not be in sin, but now you say We can see, so your sin remains.

CHAPTER 10

Indeed I tell you, indeed, the man who does not go into the sheepfold through the gate, but climbs in some other way, is a thief and a villain. But the man who comes in through the gate is the shepherd of the sheep. The gateman opens to him, and the sheep pay attention to his voice, and he calls his own special sheep by their names and he takes them to their grazing. When he has all his own sheep outside, he walks in front of them, and the sheep follow him, because they know his voice. They will never follow a stranger, they will run away from him, because they do not know the voices of strangers. Jesus told them this story, but they did not see what it was he was telling them.

So Jesus spoke to them again, Indeed I tell you, indeed I am the sheepgate. All that came before me were thieves and villains, but the sheep did not listen to them. I am the gate, if someone comes in through me, he will be saved, and come in and go out and find his grazing ground. The thief only comes to steal and slaughter and destroy. I came for them to have life, and to have more life. I am the good shepherd. The good shepherd gives his life for his sheep. The hired man is not the shepherd and the sheep are not his own, he sees the wolf coming and he leaves the sheep and runs away, and then the wolf snatches them and scatters them; because he is a hired man the sheep do not matter to him. I am the good shepherd, and I know mine, and mine know me, as my father knows me and I know my father, and I give my life for my sheep. And I have other sheep which are not from this sheepfold. I must bring them in as well, and they will listen to my voice, and they will all be one flock with one shepherd. That is why my father loves me, because I give my life in order to have it again. No one takes it away from me, but I give it freely. I have authority to give it, and I have authority to have it again; my father gave me these orders.

The Jews were divided again by these words. Many were saying, He has a devil in him, he is mad, why do you listen to him? Others were saying, The things he says do not sound like a man with a devil in him; can a devil open the eyes of the blind?

It was the festival of lamplighting in Jerusalem and it was winter. Jesus was walking in the temple, in Solomon's colonnade. So the Jews crowded all round him and they said, How long are you going to keep us waiting? If you are Christ, tell us openly. Jesus answered them, I have told you, and you do not believe me. The work I do in my father's name is my witness. You do not believe, because you are not my sheep. My sheep listen to my voice, and I know them, and they follow me. And I give them everlasting life, and they will not perish for all eternity, and no one will take them out of my hands. My father gave them to me, he is the greatest of all, and no one can take them out of my father's hands. I and my father are one. Once again the Jews picked up stones to stone him to death. Jesus answered them, I have shown you many good deeds from my father, for which one of

44

them are you stoning me? The Jews answered him, We are not stoning you for a good deed, we are stoning you for blasphemy, because you are a man and you say you are God. Jesus answered them, Is it not written in your law, I said, you are gods? If he said they were gods to whom the words of God came (and the Bible cannot be undone), do you say to one the father sanctified and sent into this world, You are blaspheming, just because I said, I am the son of God? If I do not do my father's work, do not believe me. But if I do it, then if you do not believe me, believe the work I do, so that you see and understand that my father is in me and I am in my father. They tried again to seize him, but he got away out of their hands.

And he went away again across the Jordan to the place where John used to baptize, and there he stayed. And many people came to him. And they were saying that John performed no miraculous signs, but that everything John said about Jesus was true. And many people believed in him there.

CHAPTER 11

There was a sick man called Lazaros from Bethany,
from the same village as Mary and her sister Martha. It
was Mary who rubbed the Master with sweet oil and
dried his feet with her own hair, and Mary's brother
Lazaros who was unwell. So the sisters sent to him to
say Master, look, your friend is ill. When Jesus heard he
said, This illness is not for death, it is for the glory of
God, for the son of God to be glorified through it. But
Jesus loved Martha and her sister and Lazaros. So when
he heard he was ill, at that time he stayed where he was
for two days. But after that he says to his disciples, Shall
we go to Judaea again? The disciples tell him, Rabbi,
just now the Judaeans tried to stone you to death: are
you going back there again? Jesus answered, Are there
not twelve hours in the day? If a man walks in the
daylight he does not stumble, because he sees the light
of this world, but if anyone walks in the night-time he
does stumble, because the light is not in him. That was
what he said, and then he says to them, Our friend
Lazaros has fallen asleep, I am going there to wake him.
So his disciples said to him, Master, if he has fallen
asleep he will be saved. But Jesus had spoken of his
death, and they thought he meant the sleep of natural
slumber. Then Jesus said to them openly, Lazaros has
died, and I am glad for your sake, so that you believe,
because I was not there. Shall we go to him? So Thomas

47

who was called the twin said to the other disciples, Shall we go as well, and die with him?

When Jesus came he found he had been four days already in the tomb. Bethany was near Jerusalem, about two miles away, and many of the Jews had come out to Martha and Mary, to comfort them about their brother. So when Martha heard that Jesus was coming, she went to meet him; Mary was sitting at home. So Martha said to Jesus, Master, if you had been here my brother would not have died. And even now I know that whatever you ask of God, God will give you. Jesus says to her, Your brother will rise up. Martha says to him, I know he will rise up in the resurrection on the last day. Jesus said to her, I am resurrection, I am life. Whoever believes in me will live even if he dies. And everyone who lives and believes in me will not die for all eternity. Do you believe that? She says to him, Yes, Master; I have believed that you are Christ, the son of God who has come into the world. She said it and then she went away, and called her sister Mary privately; she said, The teacher is here, he is calling for you. When Mary heard that, she got up quickly and went to him. Jesus had not arrived in the village yet, he was still in the place where Martha had come to meet him. So the Jews who were with Mary in the house and giving her comfort, when they saw her rise quickly and go out, they followed her, thinking she was going to the tomb, to cry there. When Mary came where Jesus was and saw him, she fell down at his feet. She said to him, Master, if you had been here, my brother would not have died. So when Jesus saw her crying, and the Jews who came with her crying as well, he groaned in spirit and he was troubled, and he said, Where have you put him? They said to him, Master, come and see. Jesus wept. So the Jews were saying, Look how he loved him. But some of them said, Could this man who opened the blind man's eyes not have prevented his death? So groaning within himself once again Jesus came to the tomb. It was a cave with a stone at the cave-mouth. Jesus says, Take away the stone. Martha the dead man's sister says to him, Master he stinks now. This is his fourth day. Jesus says to her, Did I not tell you that if you believe you will see the glory of God? So they took away the stone. And Jesus looked upwards and said, Father, I give thanks to you because you heard me. I know that you always hear me, but I say this for the people gathered here, so that they believe that you sent me. When he had said this, he cried out in a mighty voice, Lazaros, come out. The dead man came out, with his feet and his hands tied up in corpse-cloths, and his face was covered up in a towel. Jesus says to them, Untie him, and let him go.

So many of the Jews who had come out to Mary and saw this deed believed in him. But some of them went away to the Pharisees and told them what Jesus had done.

So the chief priests and the Pharisees summoned a meeting, and said, What shall we do? Because this man works numerous miraculous signs. If we leave him as he is, everyone will believe in him. And then the Romans will come and take our country and our nation away from us. And one of them called Kaiaphas, who was high priest for that year, said to them, You know nothing at all, you do not even consider your own interest, which is that one man should die for the people, and the whole nation should not perish. He did not say that of himself, as the high priest of that year he prophesied that Jesus was going to die for the nation, and not only for the nation, but to bring together into unity all the scattered children of God. So from that day on they plotted to murder him.

So Jesus no longer went about openly among the Judaeans, he went away from there into the country close to the desert, to the city called Ephraim, and he stayed there with his disciples. The Jewish Passover was near, and many people from the country went up to Jerusalem before the Passover to purify themselves. So they were looking for Jesus, and saying to one another as they stood in the temple, What do you think? That he will not come to the festival? The chief priests and Pharisees had given orders; anyone who knew his whereabouts was to denounce him, so that they could arrest him.

CHAPTER 12

So six days before the Passover Jesus came to Bethany, where Lazaros was. Jesus had raised Lazaros from the dead. So they made a dinner for him there, and Martha was serving, and Lazaros was one of the company with Jesus. Then Mary took a pound of precious oil of spikenard and oiled his feet, and wiped his feet with her hair, and the whole house was filled with the smell of lemons. Then Judas of Iskaria spoke, who was one of his disciples, the one who was going to betray him, Why was this scent not sold for three hundred dinars, and given to the poor? He said that not because he cared about the poor, but because he was a thief, and he had the money-box and carried what was put into it. So Jesus said, Let her alone, she can keep it for the day of my funeral. You have the poor among you for ever, you have not got me for ever.

So the vast crowds of the Judaeans realized that he was there. And they came not only for Jesus but to see Lazaros as well, whom Jesus raised from the dead. But the chief priests planned to murder Lazaros too, because through Lazaros many of the Jews went to Bethany and believed in Jesus.

The next day a vast crowd of people who had come for the festival heard Jesus was coming into Jerusalem; they took the leaves of palm trees and went out to meet him, and they cried out, Hosanna, Blessed is he that comes in

51

the name of the Lord, blessed is the king of Israel. Jesus found a little donkey and sat on it, as it was written, Daughter of Sion, do not be afraid, look, your king is coming, riding on a donkey's foal. His disciples did not realize this at first, but when Jesus was glorified, then they remembered that these things were written about him and happened to him. So the crowd of people who were with him when he called Lazaros out of the grave and raised him up from the dead were his witnesses. That was why the crowd went out to meet him, because they heard he had done this miraculous sign. So the Pharisees said to themselves, See how things are, you are doing no good at all. Look, the whole world has gone off and followed him.

Among those who came up to worship at the festival, there were some Greeks. They went to see Philip who came from Bethsaida in Galilee, and they questioned him; they said Master, we want to see Jesus. Philip comes and speaks to Andrew. Andrew and Philip come and speak to Jesus. Jesus answers them and he says, The time has come for the son of man to be glorified. Indeed I tell you, indeed, unless the grain of wheat falls into the earth and dies, it remains alone, but if it dies it brings in a heavy crop. Whoever loves his soul ruins his soul, and whoever hates his own soul in this world will keep it for everlasting life. If anyone serves me let him follow me, and wherever I am, my servant will be there too. If anyone serves me, my father will do that man honour. Now my soul is disturbed, and what can I say? Father save me from this time. But it was for this I came to this time. Father, glorify your name. And then a voice came out of heaven, I have glorified it and I will glorify it again. The crowd standing there heard the voice and they said it had thundered. But others of them said an angel had spoken to him. Jesus answered them and he said, That voice spoke for you, not for me. Today is the judgement day of the world. Today the master of this world will be thrown out. And if I am lifted up high over the earth, I will pull all the people to myself. He said this referring to the death he was going to die. So the crowd answered him, we have heard in the Bible that Christ remains for ever and ever. So what do you mean by saying the son of man must be lifted up high? Who is this son of mankind? So Jesus said to them, For a little while yet the light is among you. Walk while you have the light, or the dark will swallow you up. A man walking in the dark does not know where he is going. While you have the light, believe in the light, you will become the sons of light.

Jesus spoke these words, then he went away and hid from them. But although he had given such miraculous signs before their eyes, they did not believe in him, so that the saying of the prophet Isaiah came true, Lord, who has believed our report? And to whom has the arm of the Lord been revealed? That is why they were unable to believe, as Isaias said once again, He has blinded their eyes and hardened their hearts, in case they should see with their eyes and think with their hearts, and be converted and I should heal them. That is what Isaiah said, because he saw his glory and spoke about him. And yet all the same, many people did believe in him even among the governors. But because of the Pharisees they did not admit it, so as not to be expelled from the community and the nation. Because they loved human glory more than the glory of God.

Jesus cried out and he said, Whoever believes in me does not believe in me but in him who sent me. And whoever sees me sees him that sent me. I am light, I came into the world so that no one who believes in me is left in darkness. And if anyone hears the things I say and does not abide by them, I do not judge him. I have not come to judge the world, I have come to save the world. The man who refuses me and rejects what I say has his judge already; the words I have spoken will judge him on the last day. Because I have not spoken on my own account, but my father who sent me commanded me how to speak and what to say. And I know that what he commands is everlasting life. So the things I say, I say them as my father spoke them to me.

CHAPTER 13

Before the Passover festival, Jesus knew that his time had come to depart from this world and go to his father, and having loved his own in the world, he loved them to the end. And after supper, when the devil had already put it into the heart of Judas son of Simon of Iskaria to betray Jesus, knowing that his father had put everything into his hands, and that he came from God and was going back to God, Jesus rose from the table and put off his clothes and took a cloth and tied it round his waist. Then he poured water into a basin, and he began to wash the feet of his disciples and dry them with the cloth that was tied round him. He came to Simon Peter. Peter said to him, Master, are you to wash my feet? Jesus answered him and he said to him, You do not know what I am doing now, but later you will understand. So Peter said to him, You shall never, never wash my feet. Jesus answered him, If I do not wash you, you shall have nothing in common with me. Simon Peter said to him, Not only my feet, but my hands and my head. Jesus said to him, Someone who has been bathed needs nothing washed except his feet, he is all clean. And you are clean, but not all of you. He knew who had betrayed him. That was why he said, You are not all clean.

So when he had washed Peter's feet and put on his clothes and lain down again, he said to them, Do you understand what I have done to you? You call me the teacher and the master, and you are right because so I am. So if I washed your feet and I am the master and the teacher, you ought to wash one another's feet as well. I have given you an example, for you to do as I have done to you. Indeed I tell you, indeed, a slave is no greater than his master, and someone sent is not greater than who sent him. If you know all this, then you are blessed men if you carry it out. I am not speaking of all of you, I know the ones I picked out. But to fulfil the Bible, He who ate my bread has lifted his foot to kick me. I am telling you now before it happens, so that when it does happen you will believe what I am. Indeed I tell you, indeed, whoever takes in someone I send takes me in, and whoever takes me in takes in him that sent me.

When Jesus had said this he was disturbed in his spirit, and he made a declaration. He said, Indeed I tell you, indeed one of you will betray me. His disciples stared at one another, at a loss as to which one he meant. One of the disciples was lying beside Jesus on the same couch, because Jesus loved him. Simon Peter gives him a nod, and says to him, Tell me who he means. This disciple leaned his head on Jesus' breast and said to him, Master, who is it? So Jesus answers, I will dip a piece of bread and give it to him. So he dipped the bread and picked it up, and he gave it to Judas the son of Simon of Iskaria. And after the bread at that moment Satan entered him. Jesus said to him, Do it quickly. None of them at the table understood why he said that to him. Some of them thought because Judas had the moneybox Jesus was saying, Buy what we need for the festival, or telling him to give something to the poor. So he took the

56

piece of bread, and went straight outside. It was night.

So when he had gone out, Jesus said, Now the son of man has been glorified, and in him God has been glorified. My children, I am still with you for a little while. You will look for me, but just as I said to the Judaeans, You cannot come where I am going, so I say the same to you now. I am giving you a new command, to love one another. To love one another as I have loved you. This is how everyone will know that you are my disciples, if you keep your love of one another.

Simon Peter said to him, Master, where are you going? Jesus answered, Where I am going you cannot follow me now, but you will follow me later. Peter said to him, Master, why can I not follow you now? I will give my life for you. Jesus answered, Will you give your life for me? Indeed I tell you, indeed, you will disown me three times before the cock crows.

CHAPTER 14

Do not be disturbed in your hearts. Believe in God, and believe in me. There are plenty of rooms in my father's house. If not, I would have told you. Because I am going to prepare a place for you. And if I go and prepare you a place, then I shall come back and take you away to be with me, so you will be where I am. And you know the way to where I am going. Thomas says to him, Master we do not know where you are going; how can we know the way? Jesus says to him, I am the way, I am truth, I am life; no one comes to my father except through me. If you had recognized me, you would have known my father as well; now from this time onwards you do recognize him and you have seen him. Philip says to him, Master, show us your father, and that is enough for us. Jesus says to him, Have I been with you such a long time Philip, and still you have not recognized me? Whoever has seen me has seen my father; how can you say, Show us that father? Do you not believe that I am in my father and my father is in me? The things I say to you are not spoken on my own account; my father lives in me, he does his own work. Believe me, I am in my father and my father is in me. Or if not, then believe me because of the things I do. Indeed I tell you, indeed, whoever believes in me will do the things I do, and greater things, because I am going to my father. And I will do whatever you ask in my name, for my father to be glorified in his son. If you ask for something in my name I will do it for you. If you love me, keep to my orders. And I will ask my father and he will give you someone else to plead for you, to be with you for ever and ever: the Spirit of truth. The world cannot accept that Spirit because the world does not observe or recognize it. You do recognize it because it lives among you, it will be in you. I will not leave you orphans, I am coming to you. A little while longer and the world will not see me any more, but you will see me, because I live and you will live. On that day you will recognize that I am in my father, and you are in me, and I am in you. Whoever holds on to my orders and keeps to them is the one who loves me, and the one who loves me will be loved by my father, and I shall love him and appear to him. Judas (not the Iskarian) says to him, Master, how does it come that you are going to appear to us and not to the world? Jesus answered him, and said, If anyone loves me, he will be loyal to my words and my father will love him, and we shall come to him and make our home with him. One who does not love me will not be loyal to my words, yet the words you are hearing are not mine, they are my father's who sent me.

I have told you all this while I am with you. But your advocate, the Holy Spirit that my father will send you in my name, will teach you everything, and remind you of everything I said to you. I leave you peace, I give you my peace. I give you peace not as the world gives it. Do not be disturbed or terrified in your hearts. You have heard what I said to you, I am going and I am coming back to you. If you loved me you would be glad, because I am going to my father, because my father is greater than me. And now I have told you before it happens, so that you believe when it does happen. I shall not speak much among you any more, because the master of this world is coming; he has no hold at all over me, only so that the world may understand that I love my father, and I do as my father commanded me to do. Shall we get up and leave?

CHAPTER 15

I am the true vine and my father is the farmer. Any branch on me that grows no fruit, he takes away. And any branch that does grow fruit, he prunes it to grow more fruit. You are clean already through the things I have said to you. Remain in me and I will remain in you. The branch cannot grow fruit of itself unless it remains on the vine, and nor can you, unless you remain in me. I am the vine, you are the branches; if anyone remains in me and I remain in him, he will grow a harvest of fruit. Because without me you can do nothing at all. Anyone not remaining in me has been thrown away like the branch, and he has withered. And they collect those up and they throw them in the fire, and they burn. If you remain in me, and the sentences I have said remain in you, then ask whatever you want, and you will get it. My father has been glorified in this: that you should carry plenty of fruit, and you shall be my disciples. I have loved you just as my father loved me: stay in my love. If you carry out my orders, you will be in my love.

As I have carried out my father's orders, and I am still in his love. I have told you this so that my joy will continue in you, and your joy will be perfect. This is my law: love one another as I loved you. No one has more love than this: for a man to give up his life for the sake of his friends. You are my friends, if you carry out the laws I am giving you. I am not calling you slaves any more, because a slave does not know what his master is doing. But I have called you friends, because I let you know everything I heard from my father. You did not pick me out, I picked you out, and I have set you to go and grow fruit, and for your fruit to survive, so that my father gives you everything you ask in my name. This is the law I give you, love one another. If the world hates you, understand that it hated me before you. If you came from the world, then the world would love its own kind. But because you are not from the world and because I picked you out from the world, the world hates you. Remember what I said to you, The slave is no greater than his master. If they persecuted me, they will persecute you as well. If they did what I told them then they will do what you tell them. They will do all these things to you for my sake, because they do not know the one that sent me. If I had not come and spoken to them, they would have been sinless, but now they have no excuse for their sin. Whoever hates me hates my father as well. If I had not done miracles among them such as no one else has ever done, they would be sinless. But now they have seen, and they have hated me and my father as well. So that the words written in the Bible about them are fulfilled. They hated me for nothing. But when that advocate comes whom I shall send you from my father, I mean the Spirit of truth that comes out from my father, he will be my witness. And you are witnesses as well, because you have been with me from the beginning.

CHAPTER 16

I have told you all this so that you are not scandalized. They will expel you from your community and your nation. The time is coming when any man who murders you will think he does a service to God. They will do these things because they have not recognized my father or me either. I have told you all this so that when its time comes you remember it, because I said it to you. I did not tell you these things from the beginning, because then I was among you. But now I am going to the one who sent me, and none of you asks Where are you going? Yet because I have told you these things your hearts are full of grief. But I am telling you the truth, it is in your interest for me to go away. Unless I go away, the advocate will not come to you, but if I do go I will send him to you. And when he comes he will prove the world wrong about sin and about justice and about judgement: about sin, because they do not believe in me, about justice because I am going to my father and you will not see me any more, and about judgement, because the master of this would has been condemned. I still have a lot to tell you, but you are not able to bear it now. But when he comes he is the spirit of truth and he will guide you into the whole truth. He will not speak from himself, he will say what he hears, he will tell you what is coming. He will glorify me, because he will receive things from me, and tell them to you. Everything my father has is mine; that is why I said he takes from me and he will tell you. In a little while you will not see me any more, and then another little while and you will see me. So some of his disciples said to one another, What is this he is telling us, In a little while you will not see me any more, and then another little while and you will see me? and, Because I am going to my father? So they were saying, What does he mean by this little while? We do not know what he is talking about. Jesus saw that they wanted to question him, and he said to them, Is this what you are asking one another? Because I said, In a little while you will not see me any more, and then another little while and you will see me? Indeed, I tell you, indeed, you will weep and lament but the world will be glad. You will grieve, but your sorrow will turn to gladness. When a woman is bearing a child she feels pain, because her time has come, but when her child is born, she does not remember the pain any more, because of her gladness that a human being has been born into this world. So you have your grief now, but I shall see you again, and your hearts will be glad, and no one will take your gladness away from you. And on that day you will not ask me for anything. Indeed I tell you, indeed, if you ask my father for anything, he will give it to you in my name. Ask, and you will receive, and be completely joyful.

I have told you these things in likenesses and in stories. The time is coming when I will not talk to you in stories any more, but I shall tell you about my father in plain speech. On that day you will ask for things in my name, and I am not telling you I shall go to my father about you; my father loves you himself, because you have loved me, and you have believed that I came from my father. I came from my father into this world; I am leaving the world again, and going back to my father.

His disciples said, You see, now you are talking in plain and open words, and not telling any story. Now we know that you know everything, and you have no need to ask any question. That is why we believe that you came from God. Jesus answered them, Do you believe now? Look, the time is coming, the time has come, when you will scatter and separate, and leave me alone, and yet I am not alone, because my father is with me. I have told you all this so that in me you can have peace of spirit. In the world you are in pain, but be brave, I have overcome the world.

CHAPTER 17

After saying these things Jesus fixed his eyes on heaven and said, Father, the time has come, glorify your son, and your son will glorify you, just as you have given him power over every human creature, so that he shall give everlasting life, to recognize you the only true God, and Jesus Christ your messenger. I have glorified you on earth, I have finished the work you gave me to do. And now glorify me, father, in that glory with you I had with you before the world was. I have revealed your name to those you gave me from the world: they were yours, and you gave them to me, and they have kept to your teaching. Now they understand that everything you have given me comes from you; because I gave them those sentences you gave me to say, and they accepted them, and they truly understand that I came from you, and believed I was your messenger. I am asking for their sake, I am not asking for the world's sake, but for those you have given me, because they are yours, and everything of mine is yours and yours is mine; and I have been glorified in them. And now I am not in the world any longer, and these men are in the world, and I am coming to you. Holy father, keep them in your own name, give them to me in your own name, to be united as we are united. While I was with them I kept them in your name, as you gave them in your name; and I guarded them, and none of them was destroyed except for the son of destruction. But now I am coming to you, and I am saying all this in the world, so that they shall have my joy fulfilled in them. I have given them your teaching, and the world hated them, because they are not from the world, just as I am not from the world. I am not asking you to take them out of the world, but to keep them from evil. They are not from the world, just as I am not from the world. Consecrate them with the truth, your teaching is the truth. As you sent me out into the world, I also sent them out into the world. And for their sake I consecrate myself, so that they also will be consecrated with truth. I am not asking you only for them, but for those who believe in me through their teaching, for them all to be one as you are in me father, and I am in you, so that the world will believe I was your messenger. And I have given them the glory you gave me, to be one as we are one: I in them and you in me, so that they are made wholly one, and the world will understand that I was your messenger, and that you loved them as you loved me. Father, I want those you gave me to be with me where I am, to see my glory which you have given me, because you loved me before the world was built. Just father, the world has not understood you, but I understood you, and these men understood I was your messenger. And I taught them your name and I shall teach it, so that the love you loved me with is in them and I am in them.

CHAPTER 18

When Jesus has said these words, he went away with his disciples across the Kedron stream to where there was a garden, and he and his disciples went in. But Judas who betrayed him knew the place, because Jesus and his disciples often met there. So Judas fetches out the guard and some servants of the chief priests and the Pharisees, and he comes to the place with lights and burning torches and with weapons. Jesus knew everything that was going to happen to him; he went out to them and he said, Who are you looking for? They answered him, Jesus of Nazareth. Jesus says to them, That is me. And Judas who betrayed him was standing with them as well. Then, when he said to them That is me, they drew back and fell to the ground. So he asked them again, Who are you looking for? They said, Jesus of Nazareth. Jesus answered, I told you that is me, so if you are looking for me, let these men go. So that the words he had said should come true. I have not lost any of those you gave me. Simon Peter had a heavy knife and drew it out, and he struck a slave of the chief priest and cut off his right ear. The slave was called Malchos. So Jesus said to Peter, Put that knife away in its sheath; shall I not drink the cup my father has given me?

So the guard and their officer and the Judaean servants arrested Jesus and roped him, and first of all they took him to Annas. Annas was father-in-law to Kaiaphas, who was the chief priest of that year. It was Kaiaphas who advised the Jews it was in their interest for one man to die for the whole people.

But Simon Peter and another disciple followed Jesus. The chief priest knew this other disciple, and he went with Jesus into the chief priest's courtyard; Peter stood at the door outside. So this other disciple the chief priest knew went outside and spoke to the servant at the door, and brought Peter in. Then the girl at the gate says to Peter, Are you another of this man's disciples? He says, No, I am not. The slaves and servants were standing round a charcoal fire they had, because it was freezing cold, and they were warming themselves. And Peter was standing with them, warming himself.

So the chief priest asked Jesus about his disciples and about his teaching. Jesus answered him, I have spoken openly to the world. I have always taught in synagogue, and in the temple where all Jews come together, and I have said nothing secretly. Why do you ask me? Ask those who heard me what I said to them; look, these men know what I said. When he said this, one of the servants standing near gave Jesus a slap in the face and said, Is that any way to answer the chief priest? Jesus answered him, If I spoke wickedly, make a statement about the wickedness; if I spoke well, why hit me? So Annas sent him away still roped to Kaiaphas the chief priest.

Simon Peter was standing and warming himself. So they said to him, Are you not another of his disciples? He denied it and said No, I am not. A slave of the chief priest, a cousin of the one whose ear Peter had cut off, said, Did I not see you with him in the garden? So Peter denied it again, and suddenly they heard the cock crowed.

So they took Jesus from Kaiaphas to the governor's palace; it was early morning, and they stayed outside the palace so as not to be defiled, so that they could eat their Passover supper. So Pilate went outside to them, and he said, What charge are you bringing against this man? They answered him, and they said, If this man had not been a villain, we would not have handed him over to you. So Pilate said to them, Take him yourselves and judge him by your own laws. The Jews said to him, We are not allowed to kill anyone; so that the words Jesus had spoken should come true, about what kind of death he was going to die.

So Pilate went back inside the palace, and summoned Jesus and said to him, Are you the king of the Jews? Jesus answered, Are you asking that yourself? Or have other people told you about me? Pilate answered, Am I a Jew? Your own nation and your chief priests handed you over to me, what have you done? Jesus answered, My kingdom does not belong to this world; if my kingdom did belong to this world, then my servants would have fought, to prevent me from being handed over to the Jews. But my kingdom is not here. So Pilate said to him, Then you are a king? Jesus answered, It is you who say I am a king. I was born for this, and I came into the world for this, to be a witness for the truth. Everyone who belongs to truth listens to my voice. Pilate says to him, What is truth?

When he had said that, he went out to the Jews again, and he said to them, I can see nothing criminal in him.

But you have the custom that I should release one man at every Passover. Do you want me to release you the King of the Jews? Once again they shouted, and said, Not this man, Barabbas! Barabbas was a bandit.

CHAPTER 19

So then Pilate took Jesus and flogged him. And the
soldiers twisted a narrow crown of thorny branches and
put it on his head, and they dressed him in a purple
wrap. And they approached him and said, God save the
king of the Jews, and slapped him in the face. And
Pilate went out again, and he said to them, Look, I am
bringing him out to you, so that you understand I can
see nothing criminal in him. The Jews answered him,
We have a law, and by that law he ought to die, because
he claimed he was a son of God. So when Pilate heard
them say that, he was all the more frightened. And he
went back into the palace and said to Jesus, Where do
you come from? But Jesus gave him no answer, so Pilate
said to him, You will not speak to me? Do you not know
that I have authority to set you free and I have authority
to crucify you? Jesus answered him, You would have no
authority over me if you were not given it from above, so
the person who handed me over to you has committed
the bigger sin. From that moment Pilate tried to set
Jesus free, but the Jews shouted, and said, If you release
this man you are no friend to Caesar. Anyone who
claims to be a king is against Caesar. So when he heard
these words, Pilate brought Jesus outside and sat on a
platform in a place called the pavement, in Hebrew
Gabbatha. It was the day before the Passover, the time
was about midday. And he said to the Jews, Look, here

is your king. So they shouted, Take him away. Take him away. Crucify him. Pilate said to them, Shall I crucify your king? The chief priests answered. We have no king but Caesar. So then he handed Jesus over to them to be crucified.

So they took Jesus, and he went out of the city carrying his own cross to the place named after a skull, which in Hebrew is called Golgotha. There they crucified him, and two others with him, one on either side and Jesus in the middle. Pilate wrote a notice as well, and put it on the cross. It read, Jesus of Nazareth, the king of the Jews. Many Jews read this notice, because the place where Jesus was crucified was close by the city, and it was written in Hebrew, in Roman and in Greek. So the chief priest of the Jews said to Pilate, Do not write, The king of the Jews; write that he said, I am king of the Jews. Pilate answered, What I have written I have written. So when the soldiers had crucified Jesus, they took his clothes, and made four shares out of them, one for each soldier, and the tunic. The tunic was seamless, it was woven in one piece from top to bottom. So they said to each other, Let us not tear that, let us draw lots for that, to see who gets it. So that the Bible should come true, where it says, They divided my clothes between them and they tossed up for my clothing. That is what the soldiers did. But Jesus' mother and his mother's sister Mary the daughter of Klopas, and Mary of Magdala, were standing beside the cross. So when Jesus saw his mother, and the disciple that he loved standing by her, he says to his mother, Lady, look, your son. Then he says to the disciple, Look, your mother.

And from that moment the disciple took her for his own.

After that, knowing that everything had been fulfilled, to fulfil the Bible Jesus said, I am thirsty. A pot full of rough wine was lying there. So they stuck a sponge full of the wine on a wild marjoram bush, and put it to his mouth. And when Jesus had taken the rough wine he said, It is fulfilled, and he bowed his head and then gave up his soul.

That day was the day before Passover. So to prevent the bodies being left on crosses over the Sabbath, because that Sabbath was a great festival day, the Jews asked Pilate for the legs to be broken and the bodies taken away. So the soldiers came and broke the legs of the first man, and the legs of the other man who was crucified with him. But when they came to Jesus, as they saw he was dead already, they did not break his legs; one of the soldiers stabbed his side with a spear, and blood and water ran down from it at once. And the one that saw this happen has given evidence and his evidence is true; and he knows he is telling the truth, so that you will believe it as well. Because these things happened for the Bible to come true. Not one of his bones will be broken. And again another part of the Bible says, They will look at him that they pierced.

After all this Joseph of Arimathaea, who was a disciple of Jesus, but a hidden one for fear of the Jews, asked Pilate if he could take away Jesus's body, and Pilate gave permission. So he went and took away his body. And Nikodemos went as well, who had come to Jesus during the night at first; he took with him a hundred pounds weight of scented ointment made from bitter aloes and from the gum of bitter trees. So they took the body of Jesus and tied it up in wrappings with the spices, as the Jewish custom is at the burial of the dead. There was a garden in the place where he was crucified, and in the garden was a new tomb where until then no one had been put. So because of the evening before the Jewish feast, and this tomb being close by, they put Jesus in it.

CHAPTER 20

In the early morning before dawn on the first day after the Sabbath, Mary of Magdala comes to the tomb, and she sees the stone taken away from the tomb. So she comes running to Simon Peter and the other disciple that Jesus loved, and she says to them, They have taken the master out of the tomb and we do not know where they have put him. So Peter and the other disciple went out of the city and came to the tomb. The two of them ran together but the other disciple ran on quicker than Peter, and he got to the tomb first. And he bent down and saw the wrappings lying there; but he did not go inside. Then Simon Peter came along after him and went inside the tomb. And he sees the wrappings lying there and the towel that had been over his head. That was not lying among the wrappings, it was folded up in a place by itself. So then he went into the tomb, and so did the other disciple who got there first, and he saw and he believed. Because he had not understood the Bible yet, which says He must rise up from among the dead. So these disciples went away again to the others.

But Mary was standing outside the tomb crying, and as she cried she bent down into the tomb, and she sees two angels sitting there dressed in white, one at the head and one at the feet where Jesus's body lay. And they say to her, Lady, why are you crying? Who are you looking for? She says to them, They have taken away my master, and I do not know where they have put him. As soon as she had spoken these words she turned round, and she saw Jesus standing behind her, but she did not understand that it was Jesus. Jesus says to her, Lady, why are you crying? Who are you looking for? Thinking it was the gardener, she says to him, Sir, if it was you who took him, tell me where you put him, and I will take him away. Jesus says to her, Mary. She turns round and she says to him in Hebrew Rabbouni, which means Teacher. Jesus says to her, Do not hold on to me, I have not gone up to my father yet. Go to my brothers and say to them, I am going up to my father and your father and my God and your God. Mary of Magdala goes to the disciples and tells them, I have seen the master, and that he said those words to her.

In the evening of the same day, which was the first day after the Sabbath, when the doors of the place where the disciples were had been shut for fear of the Jews, Jesus came and stood in the middle of them, and he says to them, Peace to you. As my father sent me, so I send you. When he had said that, he breathed on them, and he said, Receive the holy spirit. If you take away people's sins, their sins are taken away from them; if you ever leave their sins upon them, their sins remain.

Thomas who was called the twin was one of the twelve, but he was not with them when Jesus came. So the other disciples said to him, We have seen the master. He said to them, unless I see the marks of the nails in his hands, and put my finger into the marks of the nails, and put my hand in his side, I am not going to believe.

And eight days later his disciples were indoors again,

80

and Thomas was with them. Jesus came with the doors shut, and he stood in the middle of them and said, Peace to you. Then he says to Thomas, Bring your finger over here and look at my hands. And bring your hand and put it in my side, and believe, do not disbelieve. Thomas answered him, and he said, My master and my God. Jesus says to him, You have believed because you have seen me; blessed are those who did not see and still believed.

Jesus performed many other miraculous signs in the presence of his disciples, which are not written down in this book. But these have been written down for you to believe that Jesus is Christ the son of God, and by believing that to have life in his name.

CHAPTER 21

Afterwards Jesus showed himself to his disciples again by the sea of Tiberias; he appeared like this. Simon Peter, and Thomas who was called the twin, and Nathanael from Kana in Galilee, and the sons of Zebedaios, and two more of his disciples were all together. Simon Peter says to them, I am going fishing. They say to him, We are coming with you as well. They went out and climbed into the boat, and they caught nothing all that night. Early morning had already come, when Jesus stood there on the beach. So Jesus says to them, Boys, have you got anything to eat? They answered No. He said to them, Throw your net on the right of the boat, and you will find something. So they threw the net, and at once it took such a mass of fish they were not strong enough to drag it in. So the disciple Jesus loved says to Simon Peter, It is the master. So when Simon Peter heard it was the master, he knotted what he was wearing round his waist, as he was stripped already, and flung himself into the sea. The other disciples came in the boat, since it was not far from land, only about a hundred yards; they were dragging the net full of fish. So when they got to dry land, they saw a charcoal fire on the ground, and food cooking on it, and bread. Jesus says to them, Come here and have breakfast. But none of the disciples had the boldness to question him, Who are you? They knew it was the master. Jesus come and picks up the bread and gives it to them, and the same with the other food. And now this was the third time Jesus appeared to his disciples after he rose up from among the dead.

So when they had eaten, Jesus says to Simon Peter, Simon son of John, do you love me more than the others do? He says to him, Yes master, you know I love you. He says to him, Graze my lambs. He says to him again a second time, Simon son of John do you love me? He says to him, Yes master, you know I love you. He says to him, Herd my sheep. He says to him for the third time, Do you love me? And he says to him, Master you know everything, you know I love you. Jesus says to him, Graze my sheep. Indeed I tell you, indeed, when you were young you tied on your belt and you went about wherever you wanted, but when you are old you will stretch out your hands and someone else will tie you and take you where you do not want to go. He said that hinting by what kind of death he was going to glorify God. And having said that he says to him, Follow me. Peter turned and saw the disciple that Jesus loved following behind, the one who lay by Jesus's breast at supper, and who said, Master, who is going to betray you? So when Peter saw him, he says to Jesus, Master, what about him? Jesus says to him, If I want him to wait until I come, what has that to do with you? You follow me. So the word went round among the brothers, that this disciple would never die. But Jesus did not say to him he would never die, he said, If I want him to wait until I come, what has that to do with you?

This is the disciple who is witness to all these matters,

the same one who has written this book; and we know that his evidence is true.

And there are many more things that Jesus did, which if they were all written down one by one, I do not think the world would be big enough for all the books that would be written.